Hutsulka

RIVER PAW PRESS

Hutsulka
Copyright © River Paw Press, 2026

First Edition: 2026

ISBN: 979-8-9896607-4-2

Poems
Copyright © 2026 Nicole Yurcaba

Layout and Book Cover Design © Silent River
Cover Art © Silent River

River Paw Press

USA

www.riverpawpress.com

Hutsulka

Nicole Yurcaba

Acknowledgements

"Ode to a Man Who Will Not Date Me Because I Do Not Look Like an American Supermodel" was named "Best Submission of 2023" by University of Saskatchewan's *The Fieldstone Review.*

"Ode to Drinking at QXT's in Newark with Franz Kafka" was published in *One Art* (2023).

"Ode to a US Army Special Forces Soldier Educating Me about My Homeland's Literature" was published in *One Art* (2023).

I am very grateful to Dr. Kristina Marie Darling, Jeffrey Levine, and everyone else at the Fall 2023 Tupelo Manuscript Conference who provided insightful feedback for this manuscript.

Table of Contents

**Ode to a Man Who Will Not Date Me Because
I Do Not Look Like an American Supermodel**

I ride horses the way my great-grandmother rode:
legs & skirt spread
my *kyptar* & *vyshyvanka* a newly discovered star
reins in one hand   my other hand on my hip
this sea of mountains the chorus forming
the song of my self
                              & my ancestors
& the stream runs cool on the horse's hooves
unlike the way your tongue roughs up
my unpronounceable name
clean-cut in my own nearly extinct language.

What's wrong with yours?

This horse's movements are mine
& mine are its & in these mountains
my voice echoes across centuries
you don't realize happened. I light
my great-grandmother's wooden pipe
as I stare into twilight's blurring pink-purple.
I straighten my back & find the brightest star
hung above my disappearing village.

Ode to Drinking at QXT's in Newark with Franz Kafka

A friend advises I stay wary
of the Existentialists. He knows
damn well I am in too deep
with Kafka, who sits beside
me on a Saturday night,
sipping a cosmopolitan.
Franz, I say. *We were born*
beautifully dead inside.
Kafka weighs our insignificance
in his right hand.
Your heart weighs an ounce
too little, Franz says. *You*
are awarded the precipice's edge.
The DJ spins Blutengel's
"Forever Young." My phone
Buzzes–a message from my friend:
Nikola, I wish you didn't think
of yourself as other. Kafka's drink
trembles in his hand. He leans
into me, his lips hot on my ear.
His finger's cold sinks through
my fishnets. *We spend too much*
time together, Franz states.
Another night, and I may not
be able to keep myself
from pushing you. I take
Kafka's hand, lead him
to the dancefloor, place his hands
on my chest. His fingers
tap   tap   tap
the bass rhythm
the policy of truth
known only by the darkness
thrumming beneath my bodice's ties.

Ode to a Man Who is the Wolf About Which He Warns

I'm in hot hot heat with a man
who quotes Kierkegaard while sipping
1792 by a fireplace & clicking "like"
on photos of half-naked girls selling
skin for my homeland's army. Three months ago,
he told me, *Our conversations reveal
your beauty.* It's Friday night in New Jersey:
two glasses of wine leave my face in a slice
of New York cheesecake. The waiter asks
if I need more water. There's a war in my
homeland. I haven't heard from my cousin
serving in the army in two days. The man
who quotes Kierkegaard jokes about grabbing
my head & forcing me to look forward, says he'll
be gentle the first few hundred times. From men,
since my teens, it's the same lines:
I love you.
I won't hurt you.
You're beautiful.
I can help you heal.
Always, the same conclusion: a flash of nipple
            a flick of thin abdomen
            the slow cry of an ass cheek's curve
            a hastily sent note– *You're great & smart,
            but…*

Ode to the Orchard Keeper

Late October: the creek facing the farmhouse is dammed
by oak leaves & fallen black walnuts, sticks & limbs
dropped by a northern wind's brashness. The air smells
of creeping black ants, dehydrated black snakes,
& Type O Negative songs. There is a war
in my homeland. The sun settles into your crow's
feet, the faint stubble cascading your cheek.
Oil, dirt, wood, apples emerge from your shirt's flannel
& I breathe in the whiskey from your breath–a gentle reminder
of our humanity in this world where five hours ago
a stranger who doesn't know me called me *Fascist Nazi scum*
for wearing my homeland's flag. Leaves slow-crunch
beneath our dirty work boots' soles.

With you, I leave the war
behind. It fades into cascading light
covering rocks peaking through browning grass.
With you, I return to my homeland:
safe despite the thirteen-hour flight. In a quaint village
my grandfather plays his *telenka* & my father
dances *arkan* while my grandmothers & mother cook.
With you, I return to my childhood's language–
sanctity & prayer & catechism & ritual–
  Oh, holiness–
  Oh, dying syllables–
  Oh, divine exorcism at my weakest hour–
  Oh, you–

Ode to the Man Who Smiles at Me across the Room at a Spanish Restaurant

The dim lights might betray me
as the waiter pours more water
from a sweating glass bottle.
My assumption: one handsome man
dining with another, conversation
minimal– first date? Business partners?
Friends? Brothers? Cousins? You're a Virginia
poet specializing in the Tang poets who asked
me four years ago *Why do you dress so weird?*
Or a financial advisor planning a client's
dwindling portfolio confused by a modern
woman wearing a fascinator & corset.
From the in-ceiling speakers, Spanish
dance music overtakes what you're saying
to the man opposite you. You glance at me,
the televised football game reflecting
in your small-framed glasses. Peas
& yellow rice tremble on my fork,
their warmth a half-light
                    reddening my lips.

Ode to a US Army Special Forces Soldier Educating Me about My Homeland's Literature

Tell me again how you want to fight
Zabuzhko's sentences into philosophies
bound by proper punctuation. You don't know
what it is like spending your life lost
in translation, how one language wrestles
a second or third face-down into mud
& forces it to swallow handful after handful–
dirt, grass, gravel, piss, shit, & blood
until you no longer remember
how to say *bird* or *sky* or *death*,
so you could wake up one day to learn
your pregnant cousin who stayed behind
in your family's homeland burned alive
in a car bombed by occupiers who clip
phone wires & mail them home believing
the internet's entirety exists within. Tell me
again my homeland's history, how our nation's
bard lived in exile, how when my family escaped
we had no home yet home is a mosaic
6,000 miles from where I stand, squinting
in wonder that you think *Lemko*
is merely a former team mate's surname.

Ode to the Man Who Makes Me Rethink

indulgence & frugality & self-determination.
You find me perusing pages torn
from hardcover volumes. The ragged
sheets crumble as I point to an anglerfish:
fin ray erect, crescent mouth armed.
You tell a joke I cannot hear.
My mouth slumps when you mention
the expense we pay for this transaction.
In this energy-poor environment,
will you hold this book while I caress
your cheek before I swim
into another aisle, seeking another
book offered by a different prey–
the green-eyed shark, lying arched
& motionless, extended jaw & stomach,
preparing for ambush.

Ode to a Man with Whom I am Writing

a book review of a philosophical novel
balancing classical & quantum physics
with the question *What truly matters?*
You tell me to be less Meta. I'm unsure
why my hair keeps falling into my eyes.
You say, *The apple doesn't care*
whether it's Newton or Einstein—
it simply falls.
Like Adam. Like Eve. Like the book
we're reading drops from my hands
into hot bathwater. Like the white
cloth napkin from my lap
on an awkward first date. Like your name
from my lips into conversations with my
family & friends & exes & self & God
& the fluorescent pink sticky tab
loosening from page 116. Today you
suggest freedom occurs
in the mathematical sense. I become
the prism you rotate in infinite directions.

Ode to a Man Who Says He Cannot See Me

Invisibility happens when you cannot see
beyond what society has offered you
on a magazine cover or television.
In your Twitter feed, I spy the likes of bare-breasted
twenty-somethings who do not know
how to properly punctuate contractions;
thin thirty-something singles advertising
recent divorces & one-night stands, their ex's
trash-bagged clothes. What I can offer isn't enough
to keep you: long afternoons discussing Socrates
& Skovoroda's writings, a photo of books
received via mail; a random text *Did you ever read
Wittgenstein at midnight during a thunderstorm?
Terrifying.* I can't give you
five minutes more, dear wolf. I refuse
to become the sheep you devour
while the shepherd sleeps beside a stream.

Ode to a Man Who Makes Me Feel Small & Pathetic

like a needle lost
among tangled skeins
lumped in a sewing bag.

I hide from whatever sentence
you might text next:
the criticism   *You're too sensitive*
the observation   *Your obsession with*
                       the apocalypse is suicidal
your charge   *Stop being cryptic. You'd*
                       save yourself a lot of trouble.

It's 2130. I can't concentrate
on reading Antonych.
There is a war in my homeland.
Weeks ago, you ceased telling me
Goodnight. Dormi bene. How beautiful
my eyes looked
                in photos I sent from my office.

Ode to a Man Who Wants Me to Carry the Weight

of the war in my homeland in silence. You say
you cannot speak to me. You say, *Two sides
exist* in every headline, social media post, meme,
joke. Over salami & cheese, I mention an illegal use
of incendiary bombs. You tell me my president siphons
money from the billions sent by the US government.
I tell you, *Shut up. Read a fucking book.* I wonder how,
when you hate my homeland so much you can
even tolerate me. Perhaps you don't, secretly.
Perhaps you fantasize about strangling me
while I sleep beside you, our cats nestled
between us. I don't love you anymore.
I haven't in seven years. I stay only
because you owe me fifteen-hundred dollars.

Ode to an Orchard-Keeper Who Sends Me Apples

pink ladies
individually wrapped in newspaper,
nestled one on top of another on top of another.
There is a war in my homeland.

My cousin in our village picked apples
until enemy missiles destroyed the orchard.

Knowing you touched each apple,
I eat them slowly:
          skin tight against my teeth
          taking you inside me
          bite   by   bite

Ode to a German Rock Star Who Flies My Homeland's Flag During His Band's Concerts

Is it publicity or is it sincerity? You sail
the crowd in an inflatable raft floated
by hundreds of hands: the colors
of my homeland an unraveling
democratic scroll. Sweat drips
into your kohl-smeared eyes. The backs
of your leather pant legs crease behind
the knees. Your band's lead singer never
misses a chance to make the crowd shriek.

You clench my homeland's flag in your right fist.
I see only my blood streaming
against a lead-colored sky
fishbowled by an overcrowded stadium.

Ode to a Man Who No Longer Speaks to Me

after I tell him McCarthy's latest novel
makes me think *I am fucking stupid*
while I'm eating Taco Bell & checking
casualty counts from the war in my homeland.

It's okay. I cope with the silence
by taking another bite of processed taco.
On NPR, a talk show host discusses
the increase in powder production
for weapons promised by an aid package
the political party you support votes against.

It's been four days since your last message,
nine months since you first said *Hi*.
I suppose you think I'm lonely
without you. On the contrary.
How could I miss anything more
than the sound of first snow
falling on invaders' frozen bodies
lying on icy steppes?

Ode to a Norwegian Man Who Apologizes for Calling me "Pretty"

Do you know how many weeks it has been
since a man even looked at me?
I am invisible, unnoticeable, the fat bastard bitch
who struggles to tug one-size-fits-all fishnet stockings
over her curves. Today I ate only salad & drank only water.
Today I wore my mother's beads I purchased at a street market
the last time I visited our homeland. My hair straggles
from the dented clip I snapped in place
this morning. I imagine your forehead
against mine during a sunset in Oslo,
long conversations about Eldrid Lunden's poetry
as we drive to the countryside village in which you
were raised. *No worries*, I tell you as I hear
a coworker confess *I stopped watching the news
weeks ago. It's so damned depressing.*

**Ode to a New Jersey Man Who Dates Me & Never Reveals
His Divorce is Not Finalized**

You tell me your ex is a cold, cold bitch & I think *How cliche.*
You're supposed to be a writer, editor-in-chief. Yesterday,
you fired two writers for typos in their articles. You tell me
you have the kids forty percent of the time. On our first date,
I joked *This is the part where you reveal you're actually married,
isn't it?* I never bothered googling your name. Don't let your
infidelity define you. Instead, I will blame my own vulnerability,
how we began talking–books, music, movies–after the invasion
of our homeland. I will blame the profile pic you said first
attracted you.

In some New York City bar, you're laughing with a friend:
That stupid woman. She thought I actually cared.

Ode to a Virginian Man Who Tells My Homeland to Go Fuck Itself

Andy Warhol was a Lemko. A Lemko–like me–was Andy Warhol.
I stopped believing in revision long ago, so come closer:
my paternal grandfather stared through a displaced persons camp's
barbed wire; my maternal grandfather shrank into himself in Dachau;
Operation Vistula flushed the syllables my English hides from Poland.
Allow me to drive your pick-up truck straight into the local convenience
store's gas pumps. Allow me to piss on the stars-and-bars that designate
your hate. You tread on me, not knowing I hide underground,
operating radios, sending coded messages regarding your
whereabouts & insurrections. Lean closer, Southern son.
I want to see the red on your neck.

Ode to a Former Boyfriend who Concealed His Mental Illness from Me

On this flight, there is no meal service.
In seat 19B, you will sit with
the cabin's weight pressing you into your seat
during takeoff.

Instead of a flight attendant's instructions,
you will hear only a machine gun's
rat-a-tat-tat, bullets piercing ill-built wings
& inches-thick windows & an oxygen mask
dangling out of your reach. You, my Icarus,
will plunge headfirst.

At the wreckage's edge, I will meet
You–beside a tattered leather suitcase,
a half-charred EU passport, scattered
doll parts lying in between fresh white
t-shirts & a pair of your Old Navy boxers.

My Icarus, I'll search for you–every ounce
of you–in pockmarked debris. I'll find
your right hand–severed
                         bloodied
                              trembling.

Ode to a Dead Man to Whom I Am Writing Letters

in an Italian leather journal I bought
four years ago after returning from my homeland.
Today, I write that my friend in my family's region
has electricity for only two hours per day. Air raid sirens
echo through her city's streets as she walked
to mail a package. Today I tell you
how my coworkers belittle me for being intelligent;
how I sit silently in my office, rereading text messages
you sent months ago. I asked if you'd ever read
Vasily Grossman. You answered, *Long ago.*
Two words. The conversation ended. Three days
later, I read your brief obituary. I stood in my office,
my hands shaking. January–ice coated cars, power lines,
trees. My phone auto-deleted the last voicemail
you left.

Ode to a Polish Man Who Questions Me About My Language

Is English your first language?

I don't know. It depends on the day.

My languages walked side-by-side,
held hands; ran through forests
where my homeland borders yours;
hiked, searching for fossils
in Pennsylvania coalfields; ate Italian
ice in Baltimore streets, then went to Mass
somewhere in industrial New Jersey.

My languages never hid from one another,
not even in high school Spanish
where classmates envied my trilling R's;
or in undergraduate linguistic classes
where sentence diagramming formed
ladders–adjectives, nouns, verbs,
the thought *But this is how we say it
at home.*

Ode to a New Zealand Actor Who Plays a Naval Officer from My Homeland's Enemy Country in a High-Grossing Film

You appear in a dream. The walls–
white. The air–frigid. I shiver
as your hands rest on my waist.
I want to tear the red star from your *ushanka,*
but your lips press to mine & you're whispering
You're the first & only & the last You're the first
& only & the last & you fade into shadows
too dark for my eyes & I'm yelling *Yuri, stay!*
Yuri, tell me you're staying! & then the cold
shrinks into the white walls & the white walls
become my dress & i leave the dream
unable to see the alarm clock's red stare
at 0550–the same time my cousin who resides
in my homeland texts from several time zones
in the future:
    the air raid sirens have not stopped since last night

Ode to a Poet from My Homeland with Whom I Am Sleeping

in a DC hotel room on a March Monday night
when shahid drones creep from your part
of our shared homeland to mine. I am tracing
the shrapnel scar lining your shoulder blade.
I take note of the gray writing poetry in your hair
& beard. Maybe no one else notices how many
more appeared between last year's February
& this year's. I count them the way my father
counts how many years it has been since he
last saw the sunset in our homeland. There is a war
no one but our people remembers. It disappeared
from headlines like youth disappearing from your eyes
on the day a missile struck your university, a museum,
a theater sheltering children. Before we met, I counted
the war's days using poems I'd composed as I sat
crying in my office. In three hours, you will wake, dress,
pull on your motorcycle jacket & ignore the text alerts
shaking awake your phone.

Ode to a Man Who Informs Me the War in My Homeland is a Proxy War Between Two Global Superpowers

Homeland is a word so few remember.
Every day I wear this war in mine:
a cloak of bloodshed & rape & mines
buried in fields awaiting plowing:
its weight pulls my shoulders downward
       bends my spine into an S-shape
        compresses each nerve & vertebrate
           & step forward into a painful marker
      into a painful marker   I cannot remove
      escape   slough
         onto the floor &
      step out of   despite sunlight
      reaching through my bedroom window
      at 0615 Eastern Standard Time.

Ode to a Border Guard Who Sends Me Books

Sprinkle them with my homeland's soil.
There is a war. Be careful where
you place your hand. Place the books
inside a secure envelope.
Seal the morning's scent inside.
Let it permeate the pages
holding my forgotten ancestors' voices
& journal entries from a reporter posted
where the enemy murdered a mother
    taped her baby & a grenade
to her mutilated body & a soldier from my homeland
slices the tape he lifts the child
the pink-orange horizon to the west
obscures into a silence the soldier

cannot–

Ode to a Man Who Defends Shostakovich Three Days After
An Enemy Invades Our Homeland

There is a war & you are listening
to his seventh symphony again
& you are decrying anyone who says
we shouldn't listen to Shostakovich
anymore he's part of the empire
                         brutality
                         infestation
                         massacre.
You tell me Shostakovich is one relic
you cannot forfeit but you'll replace him
with John Williams on your streaming playlist.
You suggest *Let's dance to Waltz No. 2 one final time*
before we decolonize our s(h)elves. I tell you
Prokofiev was actually born in the oblast
the enemy has been shelling for eight years;
Shostakovich maintained a complex
relationship with his government;
my grandmother listened to
Mussorgsky's "The Great Gates at Kyiv"
                                 and wept.

Ode to a Soldier from My Homeland Who Collects the Dead & Wounded

Tulips are blooming on the long-suffering land in Mariinka. —*Iryna Voichuk*

from the front line on an April day
the wind bristles through the limbs
of downed trees as you clean
dried blood from your vehicle

How long has it been since you touched your wife?
How long since you hugged your daughter?

exhaustion runs in the deep lines around your eyes
you scan the gray sky for incoming shells
I cry quietly you confess

in the tree beside you a bird lands & chirps
distant artillery racket out-noises your words
the bird   a reporter's question

You never know where they will land, you say

Your name is Valentyn.
I remember.

Ode to a Former Lover Who Impregnated His Ex-Wife While We Were Dating

Call it the return of history.
Call it opportune timing.
I discover the birth announcement
via Instagram late one Friday night
after contemplating the latest job offer.
A quick calculation reveals June
as the approximate month
of conception. In June, I was attending
a conference–writing poems about the war
in our homeland. In June, you were traveling,
supposedly, with your children–enduring
a six-hour flight delay, a reroute through
three major cities before coming to see me
the following week. Our visit never happened.
You claimed kidney stones & a family emergency.
I consoled my disappointed parents. I cried
into my hands at the bathroom sink until midnight.
Even now, I am crying at the bathroom sink:
a friend texts from our homeland: her apartment
building in flames; emergency vehicles lined
like coffins beside one another; white jets
of high-pressure water streaking the night.
In your photo, the baby smiles, her eyes squinted
into two black slits; her crocheted pink hat crooked
on her head. You'd told me last May, *We will have a son.*
We will name him Mykola Abraham, after your grandfather
& mine. Yesterday, a different friend posted a photo:
lying in the heavy cluster of rubble, a small boy
& his young mother.

Ode to a New Jersey Man Who Arrived Last May, Said He'd Return, But Never Did

Today, I wear the dress you said
was your favorite. It is one year
since your hand rested on my waist
& I felt you tremble through its fabric.

Last night, I dreamed you slept beside me
in a bed covered with maroon sheets.
When I rested my hand on your back,
you morphed into a fork-tongued serpent
covered in blinding blue-green scales.

The sky outside darkened. I recalled
the rainy afternoon you arrived
carrying two oversized bouquets of daisies
& sunflowers & roses–the first & only man
to arrive carrying hope & light in his hands,

cradling the vases like you later cradled
my head against the pillow that night

family members texted from our homeland:
There is a war. The world forgets.

We slept for two hours & at 0430
I sat on the bed's edge, asking you
Do you still want me?
& you answered *Yes*

& you pulled me into you & said
You have that morning-after glow.
At breakfast they will know

I will love you for a thousand years
& it still would not be enough time.

One year later & I am wearing
the dress you said was your favorite.
There is still a war in our homeland.
My father cried during our phone call

last night. A friend messaged:
Do you remember Bohdan?
We learned that he is dead,
killed in action. Tomorrow,
they send his body home.

Ode to a European Man for Whom I am Bleeding

& bleeding & bleeding & bleeding the gashes
on my forearms   from my split lip
                              the open wound above my brow
visible to the next door neighbors who pass me in the hall
& knock on the wall separating our apartments
signaling us to quiet our dispute during wee morning hours

we might wake the sleeping children
who have school the next day
while in my homeland there is a war
& now an air raid siren roars after a few still days
when you booked a holiday to the distant coast
& you invited me along for two weeks' respite

despite the blood continuing to pour
from the bullet wound damaging my femoral artery

no tourniquet can stop the bleeding
& I reach for you   begging
Whatever you do, don't let me die alone.

Ode to an Unstable Man for Whom I am Driving

long distances   shifting gears
one year after your disappearance
   the war in our homeland
   i live with the weight of it
      of you

every day

it's here i will stay with you
  in this forest
  i will hide you from the occupiers
   cover your mouth with my dirty bloodied hand
   & when they find us hidden in a thicket of *kalyna*
   i will push you to the ground & charge at them
   with my glittering axe & butterflies will scatter
   as you run toward the river
   as you wade the swelling river
   as you go farther & farther & farther
& i am left to drag their bodies to the barn
   douse it in precious gasoline
  –the last we had–
   & strike the match
   awaiting the light's dying
     word from the river
    the field the border
    the wind the echoes
    the sad song later played

  nothing & nowhere

Ode to a Soldier from My Homeland

Pryvit, Volodya.

Today smoke obscures the mountain
range north of my house. My eyes burn.
My sinuses drain & I can taste
the ash on my tongue. There is a war
in our homeland. Yesterday, a vlogger
reported the enemy's mining of the nuclear
power plant. Do you remember
your grandmother's story about The Bridge of Death?
How ash fell during an April night & people wondered
why snow fell so suddenly? Weeks–no days–
Later, children developed rashes & vomiting.
Their mothers wept, inconsolable: they could not
ease their children's suffering. When I fall
asleep these nights, I hear the dosimeter's
blip as what we can't see destroys the grain
another country already purchased.
Irradiated, bloated butterfish wash my dreams,
their scales glittering beneath a too-bright sun.
Before I wake, a mother straps a backpack
to her young son's back, uses permanent marker
to write a sister's name & phone number
on his jacket. She puts him in a car
with her cousin who's driving westward.
Before she closes the door, a single white
speck lands on her left cheek
above a single mole at her mouth's corner.

Ode to an Explorer Whose Submersible Implodes 1600 Feet from the *Titanic*'s Bow

Your failed expedition dominates headlines.

My grandmother used to remind me:
Our kind, they left us to die.
Only the rich
mattered.

There is a war in my homeland. Do you know
my friend Bohdan? He died in a fierce battle.
His wife & two children moved in
with his brother's wife & daughter. His brother's
wife can't find the medicine her daughter needs.
If she could, she wouldn't be able to afford it.

Meanwhile, people paid $250,000 to sink
toward the sea bottom in your submersible

& on the day Bohdan fell face first into
our homeland's soil, a Republican politician
declared our homeland shouldn't receive a blank check
& I received a direct deposit from my third job & i sent
the sum via PayPal to my cousin in our homeland's capital
because the mother next door lost both her boys in the East
& who will take care of us & ours if we don't verify payment
with a single click?

**Ode to My Father as I Dig Fossils in Wyoming on the 484th
Day of War in Our Homeland**

Today I chiseled prehistory. I read
the rock layers the way you read
the book about our homeland's invasion.

You say you most understand
the soldier's grief.

You are the one who suggested this
trip, a cross-country way to navigate
the weight of a sixteen-month nightmare
we call *reality*.

I call you from the quarry,
tell you in detail about the mass extinction
plate holding sixty fish in place for me
to unearth 52 million years later.

Somewhere in the area the enemy flooded,
the mud buries another human animal frying pan
leaf fence post chair sofa.

I text you a photo & the message
MASS EXTINCTION PLATE.

We haven't heard from family & friends in two days.

The world hasn't read our news in one week.

52 million years ago,
the mud settled onto these fish.

Two of them died,
heads pressed together.

Hutsulka

2025 Silent River Poetry Prize Finalist

Silent River Poetry Prize

by

River Paw Press

learn more at

RiverPawPress.Com

More from River Paw Press

One Thousand Origami Paper Cranes Fly Away
(Winner of the 2025 Silent River Poetry Prize)

by Martin Willitts Jr.

Dead Boys I Have Known
(2025 Silent River Poetry Prize Semifinalist)

by Joanna Grant

Love Letters to Ukraine from Uyava
(Winner of the 2024 Hryhorii Kochur Award, conferred by the State of Ukraine)

by Kalpna Singh-Chitnis

Also available in a bilingual English–Ukrainian edition

Любовні листи до України від Уяви

Калпна Сінг-Чітніс

Переклав

Володимир Тимчук

www.ingramcontent.com/pod-product-compliance
Lightning Source LLC
Chambersburg PA
CBHW051504140726
47987CB00006B/2877